O Wisdom

Advent Devotions on the Names of Jesus

Scripture quotations are from the New Revised Standard Version of the Bible, copyright © 1989 the National Council of the Churches of Christ in the United States of America. All rights reserved worldwide.

Psalm passages are from the Psalter in *The Book of Common Prayer*.

Forward Movement gives thanks to the music and communications ministries of Saint Mark's Episcopal Cathedral in Seattle, Washington for allowing us to reprint the bidding prayers and collects from their O Antiphon liturgy. We are also profoundly grateful for the congregation of Saint Bartholomew's Episcopal Church, Nashville, Tennessee, who offered us the use of the woodcuts on each chapter's title page, with special thanks to artists Mimi Heldman and Sally Chambers.

ISBN: 978-0-88028-471-4

Printed in USA

**Forward
Movement**
inspire disciples. empower evangelists.

O WISDOM

Advent Devotions on the Names of Jesus

Forward Movement
Cincinnati, Ohio

Table of Contents

Preface

The O Antiphons are a series of seven short sentences ("antiphons") that are recited or chanted during Evening Prayer in the days leading up to Christmas. They are familiar to most of us as paraphrased in the Advent hymn, "O Come, O Come, Emmanuel," but they have been in use in the church (and especially in monastic communities) since at least the eighth century. The recitation of the O Antiphons comes before and after the *Magnificat*, the beloved Song of Mary. Each of the antiphons begins with "O" and references one of the titles for Jesus drawn from the Book of Isaiah. Each also includes a petition that springs from this title.

December 17: *O Sapientia* (O Wisdom)—Isaiah 11:2-3, 28:29
December 18: *O Adonai* (O Lord)—Isaiah 11:4-5, 33:22
December 19: *O Radix Jesse* (O Root of Jesse)—Isaiah 11:1, 10
December 20: *O Clavis David* (O Key of David)—Isaiah 9:6, 22:22
December 21: *O Oriens* (O Dayspring)—Isaiah 9:1
December 22: *O Rex Gentium* (O King of the Nations)—Isaiah 2:4, 9:5
December 23: *O Emmanuel* (O God with Us)—Isaiah 7:14

Advent is a season of waiting, of longing with eager expectation for God's promise to be fulfilled. The O Antiphons direct our attention to the promised Messiah and build our expectation for his coming. The repeated use of the phrase "O Come" underscores our desire and enflames it. *We await the Savior*, as we anticipate his three-fold coming:

> as a child at Bethlehem on Christmas morning;
>> daily, in our own experience;
>>> and his coming again in glory, as he has promised.

There is an interesting fact associated with the O Antiphons. The first letters of each of the titles, when followed from last to first—Emmanuel, Rex, Oriens, Clavis, Radix, Adonai, Sapientia—spell the Latin words *ero cras*. This phrase means, "*Tomorrow, I will come.*" Christ has promised to come to us and to be for us all that we need. In Advent, we wait for him, look for him, expect him. *Pray your expectation and your faith in him.* He has promised to come to us, where we are, as we are.

How do you desire Jesus to come to you now, in this particular season of your life? Which name or title reflects your current desire or need? You might pray with each of these seven names but consider also other names of Jesus, such as the Good Shepherd, the Bread of Life, the Way, or the Truth and the Life. Pray your desire and expect Jesus to come to you and meet you in the place of your greatest need.

Praying with the O Antiphons is an occasion for gratitude. God has not only *promised* to come to us but *has* come to us, and for this we offer grateful thanks. How have you experienced Jesus as *Emmanuel,*

"God with us"? Have you known him as an intimate friend and companion on the way? Or has Jesus been for you *Clavis*, a "key," or *Oriens*, the "rising dawn" or "morning star," enlightening you and shedding light on your path? When has Jesus been for you *Sapientia*, "wisdom" from on high, teaching you the way to true, authentic, abundant life?

Pray your gratitude, offering a prayer of thanksgiving for all that Jesus has been and all that he has done for you.

Brother David Vryhof, SSJE
Assistant Superior
The Society of Saint John the Evangelist

About the Book

Linguistic ethno-biologists surmise that the first written prayers, prayers that are thousands of years old, match some vocal patterns of birds singing and chirping in contentment. I started crying when I heard that. There is something so beautiful about the thought of the birds of the air teaching us the song of God, something profound about the idea of us singing it back to God in the best way we know how. Some of that deep music, the soul-deep song we sing, is found in the words of Isaiah. Nowhere else in the entire Bible do we hear and repeat so many beautiful, poetic, and visceral names for God. It's no wonder that the hymn the Church has assembled from these names, the O Antiphons, carries so much emotion and meaning for so many. That's why we solicited contributions for this Advent devotional from people across the church. Through essays and poetry, art and photography, people joined the chorus.

Songs of thanks and praise, of lament and longing, of restoration and return have been on our lips for millennia. Calling out to the Living God, reminding ourselves of the promises made to us, and willing ourselves to stand firm in the midst of wars, disease, destruction, conflict, and all the other terrible things we do to each other is a way of reminding ourselves of how things ought to be, of how we are to surrender to God, of the sovereignty of God's mercy and righteous justice. Isaiah gives us a mighty chorus to sing in full-throated abandon, with verses that range from torch song to the lament of an unfaithful partner, from lullaby to love song, teaching us beloved names of the Beloved.

Traditionally, we begin singing the O Antiphons on December 17, with many places offering daily services between the 17th and Christmas Day. Through this book, we invite you to enjoy these beautiful prayers and praises during all of Advent and throughout Christmastide—and not just this year, but any year. We structured the book so that you can follow along with the weeks of Advent, regardless of how long or short a particular year's season may be. You can read this book every single year—and learn new things every single time. Because there are seven O Antiphons, we invite you to begin your reflection on O Wisdom, the first Antiphon, in the week leading up to Advent.

The O Antiphons represent a way for us to sing along with this portion of the story of God, to lift up our hearts and voices along with Isaiah's and the entire company of heaven. As we focus on the personality attributes that Isaiah reveals are part and parcel of the Messiah, we sit with all our ancestors and await Jesus' coming in glory while we ponder his presence among us. It will take all of us singing together to hear the full range of notes and harmonies—and there will be key changes we don't see coming. Sometimes we may not sing well together, or we may have to step away and catch our breath, or sing through a fit of the giggles or hiccup through sobs. But sing we must.

What is true for Isaiah and the children of Israel is true for us, too. God sees us, knows us, calls us, and invites us into the kingdom by name. With the O Antiphons, we are offered the opportunity to do the same—to see God in Christ, to know and be known by him, to call and invite him into our hearts and the world.

Our prayer for you is that you will find yourself singing and praying along with this book—and with all of creation—as you welcome Jesus, who was here from the foundation of the world, dwells among us in the mystery of the Holy Eucharist and in our hearts, and who is coming in glory to make all things new.

Rachel Jones
Editor

"O Rising Sun" was created using alcohol inks on white ceramic tile. Carefully directed forced air moved the inks across the tile, resulting in a multitude of rays, outstretched and reaching. Digital editing emphasized the presence of light in the darkness.

Donna Z. Falcone

O Come, O Come, Emmanuel

O come, Thou Wisdom from on high,
And order all things, far and nigh;
To us the path of knowledge show,
And cause us in her ways to go.
Rejoice! Rejoice! Emmanuel
Shall come to thee, O Israel.

O come, Adonai, Lord of might,
Who to Thy tribes, on Sinai's height,
In ancient times didst give the law
In cloud and majesty and awe.
Rejoice! Rejoice! Emmanuel
Shall come to thee, O Israel.

O come, Thou Rod of Jesse, free
Thine own from Satan's tyranny;
From depths of hell Thy people save,
And give them victory o'er the grave.
Rejoice! Rejoice! Emmanuel
Shall come to thee, O Israel.

O come, Thou Key of David, come
And open wide our heav'nly home;
Make safe the way that leads on high,
And close the path to misery.
Rejoice! Rejoice! Emmanuel
Shall come to thee, O Israel.

O come, Thou Dayspring, from on high,
And cheer us by Thy drawing nigh;
Disperse the gloomy clouds of night,
And death's dark shadows put to flight.
Rejoice! Rejoice! Emmanuel
Shall come to thee, O Israel.

O come, Desire of nations, bind
All peoples in one heart and mind;
Bid envy, strife and quarrels cease;
Fill the whole world with heaven's peace.
Rejoice! Rejoice! Emmanuel
Shall come to thee, O Israel.

O come, O come, Emmanuel!
Redeem thy captive Israel
That into exile drear is gone,
Far from the face of God's dear Son.
Rejoice! Rejoice! Emmanuel
Shall come to thee, O Israel.

Preparing for Advent

O WISDOM, who came from the mouth of the Most High, reaching from end to end, and ordering all things mightily and sweetly: Come, and teach us the way of prudence.

The spirit of the L<small>ORD</small> shall rest on him, the spirit of wisdom and understanding, the spirit of counsel and might, the spirit of knowledge and fear of the L<small>ORD</small>. His delight shall be in the fear of L<small>ORD</small>. He shall not judge by what his eyes see or by what his ears hear.   Isaiah 11:2-3

Wisdom is one of the most ancient names of Jesus. From the very first days of the church, Christians have equated the eternal Word (John 1:1) with the Wisdom of Christ (1 Corinthians 1:17-2:13). In Wisdom, all glory, power, knowledge, and radiance of God is found.

From the moment of creation, the *Logos* or the Word of God was present, bringing all things into being. Wisdom speaks creation into being. Without Christ, not one thing was made. So to invoke Wisdom is to recall Christ's majesty from the beginning right up to our day and then to the end of all days.

We pray for prudence, the judgment to use all that God has given us for God's glory. Being prudent does not mean being cautious. Rather, if we are prudent with what God has given us, we will use it well, for the good of all.

This antiphon is a plea for Christ's coming so that we might glorify him in all that we do.

Scott Gunn

We all stand in need of wisdom these days. When truth itself is in question, contemporary society struggles mightily to recognize wisdom. Yet, with each passing day, our deep needs for wisdom and discernment in all areas of life are evident. But how do we become wise? We must begin with a desire to grow in wisdom. Our search for wisdom continues with the practice of discernment to develop character. Wisdom is sustained through daily prayer—it is a process of becoming. God is both the giver of wisdom and wisdom itself.

To desire wisdom is to seek to love God in radical ways. Wisdom allows us to see, think, speak, and do the will of God in all things. In desiring wisdom, we seek to align ourselves with actions that reveal the reign of God.

In the Jesuit spirituality that helped form me, desiring something is the first step toward discernment. Jesuits are taught the importance of desiring what is good, true, and beautiful—and leads to God's greater glory. In conversation with a friend, she mentioned she had never thought of praying for wisdom. We gave each other the challenge to begin praying for wisdom daily, to desire wisdom in discernment.

This antiphon reminds us of the seven gifts of the Holy Spirit. Wisdom contains a mosaic of gifts: knowledge, understanding, counsel, fortitude, piety, fear of the Lord. Indeed, wisdom opens many gateways to God. Let us pray more intentionally for wisdom. Let us desire wisdom in this holy season and bear witness to the love and blessings God offers to us. Let us practice the right actions that help us grow in wisdom.

From a place of wisdom, may we remember that we are
made in the image and likeness of God and called to be
God's presence in the world.
From a place of wisdom, may we remember that we are
called to serve the lost, the least, and the poor. We are
called to see God in them and be God for them.
From a place of wisdom, may we remember and believe
that whatever we do to the least, we do to God.
Wisdom invites us to see that the stranger, the prisoner,
the immigrant, the refugee, the homeless, and the poor are
God in hiding, God made manifest.
May we remember. Amen.

Mark Bozzuti-Jones

In the Roman Catholic tradition, "Seat of Wisdom" or "Throne of Wisdom" (the English translation of the Latin *sedes sapientiae*) is one of several devotional titles for Mary, the Mother of God. It describes her status as the vessel in which the Holy Child was carried. In Seat of Wisdom icons and sculptures, Mary is seated on a throne holding the Christ child in her lap. She is also the seat on which Christ, the embodiment of divine wisdom, sits.

In the early 1990s, St. Thomas Church Fifth Avenue, New York City, where I am a parishioner, received its own Seat of Wisdom sculpture, known as Our Lady of Fifth Avenue. Sculpted and cast in bronze by the late Mother Concordia, who was an English nun and artist, the work captures the serene bearing of the Madonna and the loving wisdom of the Christ Child.

Dear Lord, as we make our way through a world that is often noisy and disquieting, please help us to be as serene and steady as Mary. Help us also to seek and embrace the wisdom of her son Jesus Christ. Amen.

Pamela Lewis

I was a high school teacher for nearly three decades. I learned that wisdom and understanding are as important to being an effective instructor as being an expert in the subject area.

On a hard day, with voice raised and eyes welling, a student accused me of treating her unfairly. Taking her hands in mine, I responded calmly and suggested we meet to talk during a time convenient to both of us. In retrospect, I believe I acted wisely by deeply listening and was able to compassionately counsel my student with an understanding ear. Our relationship improved.

The Pharisees, scribes, and other powerful and clever people seek to ensnare Jesus with their *smart* questions. But Jesus is always *wise*. He puts his wisdom into action, both by disputing the experts in the temple and challenging would-be stone-throwers and through his conduct when he faces arrest, trial, condemnation, and death.

From Mary's womb to the Garden Tomb, the Spirit of the Lord rests on Jesus. It is with profound and holy wisdom, understanding, and counsel that Jesus teaches his disciples—and continues to teach us.

Dear Lord, Help me remember that your wisdom is greater than the knowledge of the world. Help me to be discerning, as well as wise, and to be guided by the mind of Jesus, not just the minds of humans. Amen. Pamela Lewis

We live in a postmodern world. We celebrate relativism and globalism, distrust history and language, and denounce capitalism and absolutism. Society professes devotion to the values of inclusion and diversity reflected in Jesus' commandment, "You shall love your neighbor as yourself" (Matthew 22:39b). Yet we live in a dystopian, dysphoric, and disoriented society. Our nightly news and social media lead with stories of fear and hate and random violence.

Thankfully, the ancients see prudence as the foundation of all virtues because it provides discernment for us to conduct our lives with courage, temperance, and justice. Just as God uses unrivaled power and transcendent love to transform elemental chaos into an ordered universe, so can our own wise choices transform the cacophony of our daily lives into perfect harmony—in our hearts and in our lives with others.

As we begin Advent, this holy season of solemn contemplation and preparation, may we realize that we can only find the peace we seek when we choose with Wisdom to lead lives in God's perfect order.

O God, who by the light of the Holy Spirit did instruct the hearts of the faithful, grant that by the same Holy Spirit, we may be truly wise and ever enjoy his consolations, through Jesus Christ our Lord. Amen.

Vicki Bozzola Derka

"O Sapientia:" This original pen and ink drawing features a goose, a Celtic symbol of the Holy Spirit—the giver of wisdom and peace–with a clutch of goslings.

Stephanie London

O WISDOM, your words spoken in the beginning of creation generated a world of beauty and goodness: Come and instruct us in the way of prudence, that we may care for your world with justice and compassion; through the one whom we know as the Wisdom of the Ages, Jesus Christ our Lord. Amen.

Advent 1

LORD and Ruler of the House of Israel, who appeared to Moses in the flame of the burning bush and gave him the law on Sinai: Come and redeem us, with outstretched arm.

Sunday

*But with righteousness he shall judge the poor, and decide with
equity for the meek of the earth; he shall strike the earth with
the rod of his mouth, and with the breath of his lips he shall kill
the wicked. Righteousness shall be the belt around his waist, and
faithfulness the belt around his loins.*   Isaiah 11:4-5

God has many names in the Old Testament, but the name most often
used is, by tradition, not pronounced by God's people. God's name is
considered so sacred that it never passes the lips of God's followers.
Early on, a custom developed to replace this unpronounceable name
with *Adonai* when reading text aloud. *Adonai* means, roughly, "My
Lords." God is so sacred that the name is plural rather than a singular.

This all sounds very heady, but what it means for us is that when
we pray for Adonai to come among us, we are invoking the majesty,
the awe, and the power of Almighty God. God pronounced this
name to Moses in the burning bush and led Moses to receive the
Law on Mount Sinai.

We Christians understand ourselves as heirs of the chosen people led
by Moses. We are asking our God, the same God who led us from
captivity to freedom in the Red Sea, from chaos into order on Mount
Sinai, from wandering to our home, to come among us and lead us
once again.

Scott Gunn

Monday

Considering what was going on in our house, it would have been all too easy to miss the moment. Up to my armpits in tape, wrapping paper, and presents, my husband Ron had very generously made me breakfast and taken our oldest child to do some last-minute errands that were "None of your beeswax, Momma!"

Just our youngest and I were at home. She was playing quietly upstairs, watching a Christmas video. Entertaining a three-year-old while wrapping presents *wasn't* on my "To Do List" for the morning, but she was being really good. She only tried twice to come into my bedroom. For someone who had recently come to understand the idea of sweet surprises, she was doing well staying on her side of the door.

I came banging up the stairs with a load of junk that had been strewn around the house, muttering about being tired of always picking up other people's stuff. "Shh," she whispered. "Momma, Baby Jesus is being born for *me*!"

There, sitting on the floor of our game room, she had cobbled together pieces of a dozen nativity scenes from around the house—Bob the Tomato and Larry the Cucumber from a *Veggie Tales* set, now dressed as a shepherd and a king and an assortment of angels with serene faces, knowing looks, and big grins. Mix-and-match cattle, sheep, donkeys and camels gathered near the makeshift manger and no fewer than four baby Jesuses jockeyed for prime position. I stood there with my mouth agape, tears in my eyes.

With Nutella spread across her cherub cheeks, she explained that the cast of characters were waiting for Jesus to be born again—this time just for her. When I asked her why she had so many tiny infants there, she looked at me as though this was a silly question and answered simply, "Because I *need* him!"

Don't we all?

Oh, sweet Baby Jesus, thank you for being born again for us today. Help us to fix our eyes on you, to silence our busy to do lists, and to wonder at your great love for us. Shift our focus to your face, not just your law. Teach us again to look to you as our righteousness and faithfulness in a world that sometimes seems so fixated on our busy lives that we have lost the "cloud and majesty and awe" of needing you more than we allow ourselves to admit.

For those who usher us into wonder with tiny hands, bright eyes, and hearts wide open: Lord, hear our prayer. Amen.

KariAnn Lessner

Tuesday

It is human nature to judge. Judging others, sizing up things and experiences, is how our brains are wired for learning and memory—this is how humans learned which plants to eat and which to avoid, which animals were friends and which ones thought of us as food. We take in information and incorporate it into categories through assimilation with what we already know and accommodation of new ideas that prove logical and convincing. While judging is a natural instinct, we must take care that we do not succumb to moral judgments and stereotypes. In Matthew, Jesus teaches that we should avoid this aspect of our human nature: "For with the judgment you make you will be judged." This is one of the hardest Christian disciplines to practice.

Striving to be like Jesus, fully human and fully divine, we seek to apply righteousness in our judgment. Striving to be like Jesus, we seek to see the heart of others. But we are merely (and only) human, and we do not see the way Jesus sees. Our natural tendency toward judgment is inevitably flawed and self-serving. We must strive mightily against our nature when seeking to emulate Christ in this way.

Self-examination seems the better focus of our judgmental tendencies but even that can become injustice. But it is precisely because of our imperfect judgment that we need the power and might of God's righteous judgment to come and abide among us.

O Sacred Lord, make haste to help us. In your righteousness, have mercy upon us. Give us grace to see with eyes like yours the heart of every person we meet. With your help, Sacred Lord, may we strive continuously for justice and peace among all people, respecting the dignity of every human being. Amen.

Elizabeth Floyd

Wednesday

The prophets would strike terror into our hearts if we listened to them. Nothing pleasant is promised to us when we blame the poor for their poverty, when we find it easy to roll up our windows and make excuses for ignoring needy people on our streets. God pronounces judgment on those of us who allow poverty and hunger to exist without remedy, calling us "wicked."

One winter day, I was rolling home from work and noticed a man sitting on the curb, head in his hands. I stopped and asked if he was okay. Quietly, almost reluctantly, he mentioned the cold in his bones and in his apartment, his empty pantry, his hunger, and his lack of money, even for bread and milk. He hardly looked up, embarrassed to be speaking so freely to a stranger.

You have a few dollars, I thought to myself. But I didn't want to give it away, even though I felt badly for him. I was cold too and had planned to stop at Taco Bell for supper. *You also aren't that darn hungry*, I retorted to my stomach. *You can always eat at home.*

The man didn't expect anything from me. We were quiet together for a few minutes as evening gathered around us. Suddenly, I knew something powerful and important: *Right here is where God intends to judge for the poor. Let God do this.*

Since I have no arms, I asked the man to pull my wallet out and take what was in there. It wasn't that much, honestly. But it was what I had. And the Holy Spirit said it belonged to him, not me.

"You're not serious," he said, glancing inside. "Yes," I repeated, "Take it all."

We went away rejoicing. Thanks be to God.

Give us today, Lord, our daily bread. And teach us to give daily bread to all who hunger every day. Amen.

Minda Cox

Thursday

God's economy
begins in this convenient
car wash; by spurting spigot,
Man fills plastic water jugs
crafted by a nameless
corporation.
Woman produces eclectic plasticware—
cubes, saucers—from ubiquitous
black garbage bag carryall.
That synthetic black loosely
clothes her corpus too,
leadenly animate in the chill.
Giving each dish a quick rinse
under the gushes, she then lays
them out on the grass.
No shame in either frame
as each performs their corporate chores.
Store's red-shirted clerk ignores
their theft.

Gas pump clicks, banishing me
from this Eden, not them.
Conveniens? I whisper, a Thomist
ghost flitting 'round
my reasoning heart.

Fitting, I murmur--
this is the wisdom of the world.

Almighty God, give us grace to cast away the works of darkness,
and put on the armor of light, now in the time of this mortal life in
which your Son Jesus Christ came to visit us in great humility; that
in the last day, when he shall come again in his glorious majesty to
judge both the living and the dead, we may rise to the life immortal;
through him who lives and reigns with you and the Holy Spirit, one
God, now and for ever. Amen.   *The Book of Common Prayer*

Christine Havens

Friday

Every year, the ramp-up to Christmas prompts acts of giving and generosity. It's the height of donation and volunteer season. Canned foods are collected, presents for children are wrapped, and checks are signed. But what other gifts can we—and should we—be giving year round? What gifts can we give that allow equality, righteousness, and justice to flourish?

As we look around and consider what the world needs, let us give our attention—and the microphone—to those needing to be heard. Let us give our presence—and show up—for those needing support. Let us give our voice—and speak up—when we witness injustice. Let us use our respective platforms and talents to advocate for others. And let us give radical love and endless compassion to all.

As the Light himself would, let us share these gifts with the passerby asking for change and with the neighbor we don't agree with. Let us give these gifts to protesting students and families torn apart. Let us give these gifts to those who don't conform to society's limiting norms and let us give to those who are systematically oppressed. Let us share our attention, our presence, our voice, our love, and our compassion with those around us.

Jesus—like us—was not born into a world of equality, righteousness, and justice, nor did he die in one. However, he spent his lifetime pursuing these ideals and teaching others to do the same. So as we tie each bow and drop our check in the mail, let us also write to our representatives, sign up for a protest, listen to each other's stories, and ask how we can be better advocates for our communities.

Let us wear righteousness—and radical love—as a belt around our waists, wherever we go.

Almighty and most merciful God, we remember before you
all poor and neglected persons whom it would be easy for us
to forget: the homeless and the destitute, the old and the sick,
and all who have none to care for them. Help us to heal those
who are broken in body or spirit, and to turn their sorrow
into joy. Grant this, Father, for the love of your Son, who for
our sake became poor, Jesus Christ our Lord. Amen.

The Book of Common Prayer

Alyssa Finke

Saturday

Upon meeting Joey, it became apparent that a combination of bad choices—made for him and by him—had led to his current situation. Equally obvious was his hunger for community. Economic opportunity passed by our old river town, leaving shuttered storefronts and thriving pill mills swirling around in eddies of generational poverty. It wasn't uncommon to have three or four people knock on the church door each day, asking for help for baby formula or diapers or money for the electric bill.

When Joey knocked, he asked if he could do some odd jobs to make money. He cleaned out closets and painted Sunday School rooms, cleared brush from the campus, and weeded flower beds. Soon he was attending church each Sunday, helping with coffee hour and playing with the kids.

One of the last times I saw Joey, he was beaming. He rolled up the sleeve of his plaid shirt to show me a new tattoo: the Lord's Prayer stretched from shoulder to wrist. Joey explained that he wanted the prayer that we said every Sunday to be with him on all the other days too.

There was no spellcheck for this tattoo. Hallowed wasn't even close, Kingdom was missing a "g," and thy will was "they well." My inner editor cringed until I thought about this tattoo in a new light—about how willing Joey was to make the Lord's Prayer a permanent and sacramental fixture on his body, a visible sign of inward change.

Joey had witnessed something transformative in the prayer that we offer to Jesus, something powerful in the way it draws together the hearts of those who pray it, toward the source of the prayer itself.

"So what do you think?" Joey asked, smiling.

"It's perfect," I said. "Just perfect."

Joey soon dropped out of our lives entirely. Rumors swirled about where he had gone—a new job? A relapse? We never knew for certain. I hope he's well—and that he knows his tattoo marked me as well. I am convicted and comforted by his witness: Wherever Joey wandered, the Lord was visibly, tangibly, with him.

Lord and Ruler of the House of Israel, come and redeem (all of) us, with outstretched arm. Amen.

Richelle Thompson

O ADONAI, ruler of the house of Israel, you rescued remnants of your people from slavery and exile: Come and with great might deliver us from all that binds us to sin and alienates us from you, through the one whom we know as Mighty Savior of all, Jesus Christ our Lord. Amen.

Advent 2

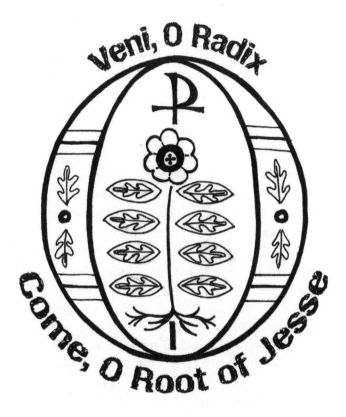

O ROOT OF JESSE, which stands for an ensign of the people; before whom the kings keep silence, and unto whom the Gentiles shall make supplication: Come and save us, and do not delay.

Sunday

A shoot shall come out from the stump of Jesse, and a branch shall grow out of his roots. On that day the root of Jesse shall stand as a signal to the peoples: the nations shall inquire of him, and his dwelling shall be glorious.   Isaiah 11:1,10

The eleventh chapter of Isaiah begins with lovely poetry, a prophetic imaging of a holy future. Jesse, of course, is the father of David. And David one of Jesus' ancestors. So it is that Christians have understood this prophetic poetry to describe the reign of Jesus. To name Jesus as the Root of Jesse is to see him in continuity with hundreds of years of divine favor among God's chosen people, as the fulfillment of all that has come before.

We are reminded that God's plan of salvation is eternal, spanning hundreds of years and generation upon generation. Not only is God's desire for our salvation timeless, but it is vast. It is for all time and all people. Though we cry out to the Root of Jesse of ancient origins, we beg Jesus to come speedily to save us.

Scott Gunn

Monday

❀ o ❀

Stumps symbolize forgotten or broken dreams, dashed hopes, and death. But God's dream to Isaiah is a reminder to him and the people of God that God does not abandon the promises of God. This root of Jesse is the root from the Garden of Eden, the tree of Life, the One who comes in the name of the Lord. God's promises are always fulfilled.

Amidst the challenges in our daily life, political challenges, wars, and deaths, something wonderful will spring up and call us to new life. But we must pay attention, or we could miss the opportunity to cooperate with what God is doing.

Those of us who have experienced cold, freezing, gray winter months know the joy of seeing spring sprouting new life. The eager lilies and crocuses push back the night soil; new shoots and branches signal the coming of spring. We who garden or pay attention to nature cannot help but marvel at how branches grow and how miraculously a lifeless trunk sends shoots toward the sun. The growth of new plants and the budding of new branches are powerful reminders that life wins. New birth and new growth signal to us that love, life, and God are ever present—in potentiality as well as in fruition.

As people of faith, we remember that things may not bloom or happen on our timetable. Things often do not come to fruition when we wish; however, no matter the delay, we are called to believe and to have faith because our God is the God of Life. Each Advent, we are called into the expectation of God's glory and the fulfillment of prophecies in Jesus Christ. Advent requires that we wait in hope, act in faith, and live in the knowledge and love of Jesus.

To wait on Jesus does not mean remaining idle, however. It means we water the gardens, do the pruning, and tend to the flourishing of our lives and others'—we do what is life giving. We cooperate with life. And we do this in whatever circumstances we find ourselves. God will meet us there. A shoot shall come out. We can rely on that.

O God, you have bound us together in a common life. Help us,
in the midst of our struggles for justice and truth, to confront
one another without hatred or bitterness, and to work
together with mutual forbearance and respect; through Jesus
Christ our Lord. Amen.

The Book of Common Prayer

Mark Bozzuti-Jones

Tuesday

I had a dream about a pathway I used to walk as a boy. This path was crooked, winding around old stumps and across a couple of creeks I could jump over if I ran like a deer down the hills. Eventually, my friends and I found just the right logs to bridge those low places. It could be a little scary in the woods as darkness fell, especially when I was traveling alone.

I think of this pathway when I read about Isaiah's dream of faithfulness, of discovering a pathway to get home safely.

The prophet does not make the pathway straight because the Lord needs it to be straight. The prophet makes the pathway straight because we sheep are prone to wander. The prophet does not fill in the valleys because the Lord needs them to be filled. The prophet fills in the low places because we can't always run like deer and land safely on the other side of the void. The prophet does not give warnings because the Lord needs the prophet to talk some more. The prophet gives warnings because sheep are notorious for becoming lost and afraid in the dark.

Who are your prophets—the men and women of God who speak to your heart? For whom will you bear the burden of prophecy? God knows we need one another on the pathway home—we need messengers to point us in the right direction. God knows we need Jesus to be the pioneer and perfecter of our faith, to give us courage and shepherd us on the journey.

Merciful God, who sent your messengers the prophets to preach repentance and prepare the way for our salvation: Give us grace to heed their warnings and forsake our sins, that we may greet with joy the coming of Jesus Christ our Redeemer, who lives and reigns with you and the Holy Spirit, one God, now and for ever. Amen.

The Book of Common Prayer

Furman Buchanan

Wednesday

For years, our family has visited my in-laws in Puerto Rico between Christmas and New Year's. We have always lived in cold places, so the midwinter break breathes much needed warmth into our bodies and souls. When the island was ravaged by hurricanes in September of 2017, we wondered what would become of our annual trip. Despite the slow response from the mainland US government, enough was up and running on Puerto Rico by December for us to make our journey.

Certainly, the island still faced serious challenges: Traffic lights were out of service, and electrical poles leaned precariously along roads and against buildings. The human cost of the slow response to this set of catastrophes and the lack of substantive support from the federal government was—and continues to be—a serious issue of justice denied. Still, we saw resurrection taking place in every corner.

Palm trees in December are always amazing to a Northerner, but we witnessed new shoots coming out of even the most bent and bowed twigs. Amidst the most punitive political and environmental challenges, the trees were winning—life was winning. Branches withstood winds of more than 100 miles per hour; these trees knew in their veins the harshness that was possible and still sent out new shoots in the most riotous, thriving shade of green I have ever seen.

As in our own lives, God can work wonders with branches we thought were dead. Winds we don't think we can withstand clear the way for new growth. Jesus, from middle-of-nowhere Nazareth, born to a poor carpenter and a young woman, comes to be the light to enlighten the entire world. Shepherds and magicians following the stars herald the savior of the world. Is there anything too wonderful for God? There is not. Not the savior who comes for everyone, not the outsiders who visit at his birth, not that astonishing shade of new green blanketing the mountains of Puerto Rico—*nothing* is too wonderful for God.

O Jesus Christ, O branch of Jesse, nurture your new growth in our lives. Amen.

Sara Irwin

Thursday

❦ ◦ ❦

Ours is an incarnational faith. I have heard this statement about the Episcopal tradition time and again. But what does it mean? Even in this period of waiting, this season of Advent, Jesus is present to us in the flesh. He lives and dies and is resurrected on this earth as a human being. Never a wispy, semi-angelic being whose experience of earthly life is merely spiritual, Jesus understands everything about this life. Here is an enfleshed God with bloodlines, appetites, and neighbors. If there is any doubt about this, the image for this week's antiphon is a root—piercing the earth, drawing sustenance from it.

Jesus comes to us as the Word made flesh—purposeful, knowable, and easy to be with. Jesus is our brother, so we do not hesitate to bypass kings and clergy to ask him for deliverance and mercy, to look to him to see how to make peace and to forgive. We are bold enough to tell Jesus to hurry up and make things right in this world.

In the Hebrew scriptures, references to the "nations" are understood as meaning Gentiles—a word for "other"—those outside the covenanted relationship with the children of Israel. Frequently, Isaiah's words draw these others into the blessing of God. Standing within the tribe of Judah, descended from Jesse and Jesse's son David, Jesus shuts the mouths of those whose speech divides people. He is rooted in this earth—he has been present from the moment of creation—he is one with us. He hears the prayers of all humankind.

Jesus, my brother, walk this earth with me. Come even today and show me the truth of this creation, of these faces that image you, of my own self who longs for you. Hear the prayers of those who cry out to you for deliverance. Amen.

Marguerite Kirchhoff

Friday

God is always making a people out of a group of nobodies, always bringing us out of bondage into freedom.

God often offers us salvation in unexpected places. We hear Gabriel's message to a teenager, pregnant under unbelievable circumstances, concerning her miraculous child, who will be born in a humble, precarious place in an occupied town.

In Isaiah's eleventh chapter, God promises us a ruler descended from King David, son of Jesse. The royal family tree may have been reduced to a stump as various armies have occupied the land, but God can make anything grow.

This vision must be a breath of fresh air to those who have been at the mercy of Egypt, Babylon, and Rome. God has promised to restore them to Jerusalem and to restore Jerusalem as the City of Peace. God's promises about today are no different.

We live in what Thomas Merton called the "time of no room." We have no room for rest or for each other or for God. We exploit each other, and the places we inhabit are often ruled by greed, hopelessness, and fear. We damage our communities and ourselves with violence and distrust.

But in Jesus, God teaches us and shows us how to love. By water and the Spirit, God pours out grace upon grace, so that we might live as brothers and sisters, be renewed and reawakened in God's image, and follow Jesus in all his ways.

Almighty and everlasting God, whose will it is to restore all things in your well-beloved Son, the King of kings and Lord of lords: Mercifully grant that the peoples of the earth, divided and enslaved by sin, may be freed and brought together under his most gracious rule; who lives and reigns with you and the Holy Spirit, one God, now and for ever. Amen. The Book of Common Prayer

Bill Carroll

Saturday

An exuberant poinsettia sits in the middle of our coffee table, reminding me that Christmas is approaching. Its green stems and brilliant red leaves evoke Christmas so thoroughly that I often forget poinsettias are actually tropical plants. They appear in my life when temperatures drop and snow begins to fall, when I'm wearing thick sweaters and drinking warm drinks. For reasons I could list and others I'm probably not even aware of, these familiar, festive plants make me feel happy.

I've tried once or twice to cultivate poinsettias after Christmas, so they could thrive again the next year. But by the middle of February, I invariably become distracted by the urgencies of the present moment rather than the beauty of what could be. The once-vibrant leaves droop, the soil dries up and cracks open, and the roots begin to shrivel. It's so complicated, this business of caring for a poinsettia outside of its symbolic season.

This is one reason why I'm grateful for the different seasons in the liturgical year. Advent reminds me to tend my roots, to wait patiently and hopefully. This preparation for the birth of Jesus prompts me to recall that even during our darkest and coldest days, new life is growing, preparing to reveal itself. Our faith does not teach us that a shoot *might* come out of the stump; it teaches us, "a shoot shall come out of the stump." Every year during this season, we are called to honor that profound guarantee, hopeful in the knowledge that God always calls forth new life, that God has become an incarnational reality, that God will—this year and next year and the one after that—create new life within us and in the world.

God of all life,
we ask you
to strengthen our roots,
cultivate our branches,
and nourish our new growth.
When we encounter hopelessness,
help us to be signs of hope,
when we meet anxiety,
heralds of trust,
when we witness despair,
beacons of joy.
Amen.

Lynn Domina

O ROOT OF JESSE, you reach deep into our hearts, drawing forth our longing for justice: Come and plant within us a passion for your Kingdom; through the One whom we know as the Root of all righteousness, Jesus Christ our Lord. Amen.

Advent 3

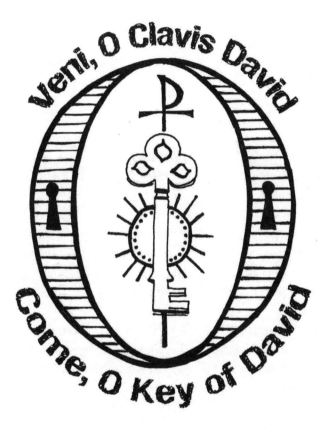

O KEY of DAVID, and Scepter of the House of Israel; who opens and no one shuts; who shuts and no one opens: Come and bring forth the captive from his prison, he who sits in darkness and in the shadow of death.

Sunday

I will place on his shoulder the key of the house of David; he shall open, and no one shall shut; he shall shut and no one shall open.

Isaiah 22:22

To call on the Key of David is to call on the one who opens and closes, who binds and releases. It is a cry for deliverance, for we know that setting captives free is a theme that returns again and again in scripture.

When Jesus was born, the Holy Land was in the grip of an oppressive military occupation. Religious authorities had been co-opted by a mighty empire. Liberation was not symbolic language, but the very real hope of a people yearning for freedom.

Today we are in captivity too. We are in captivity to consumerism, greed, fear, isolation, injustice, and oppression of many kinds. Jesus opens the door, freeing us from our sins, our fears, and all forms of captivity. Come quickly, and deliver us.

Scott Gunn

Monday

Recently, I was designing a craft for children based on Psalm 23. I started with a large loop that would hold a string of beads representing each phrase of the psalm. I attached a little suction cup to the top of the loop so it could hang on a window to catch the sunlight.

I gave thought to the shape and color of each bead so that each one could draw the children toward the Good Shepherd. "The LORD is my Shepherd; I shall not be in want" (obvious choice: a lamb-shaped bead); "he makes me lie down in green pastures" (a jade bead from the Philippines); "and leads me beside the still waters" (a clear blue bead from my local craft store); and so on.

When I finally got to "and I will dwell in the house of the LORD, for ever," I was stumped. Any dinky charm in the shape of a home couldn't possibly encompass the majesty and awe I associate with the wonder of being invited to live in God's house forever. And that's when I knew: the bead for this bit of the psalms wasn't a bead—it was a key.

I will never forget the first time my parents gave me a key to our home. I can recall the weight of that small, flat piece of metal in my pocket all day at school. I checked over and over to make sure it was still there. I imagined all the rights and privileges holding that key represented—access to our home was denied to anyone but a holder of that key, and I was one of those people.

God has placed on children's shoulders—on all our shoulders—the key to the heavenly home. It isn't clear why God chooses to place the key on our shoulders, but I wonder if that might be because that's exactly where God's hand would rest if we were walking side by side, God leading us home. God has built heaven with us in mind. Heaven is our home.

What does home sound, smell, or taste like to you? What does home look like to you? What does home feel like to you? Some say that God is in the details, and I take that as a gospel truth. I believe that God cares for our every need, loves our favorite things, and revels in our idiosyncrasies.

If ever you wonder (and you should wonder—there is so much room for imagination) what heaven will be like, be assured your heavenly home will far surpass what you can ask or imagine. God's just like that. We belong in that place; we were made for that home. We have a place of honor at that table and a key—Love its very self—to the door.

For the key in our pockets or on our shoulders that reminds us where we belong and where home truly is, Lord, hear our prayer. Amen.

KariAnn Lessner

Tuesday

O Key of David, Savior and Redeemer of Open Doors. As we try to lock you out—with our fear, prejudice, worry, and darkness—we find that our locks don't work so well. Unlock us with your Key. Give us the light, peace, and courage to open up our locked places to you and to shut the door on all that separates us from you. We build unhappy walls that divide us from our brothers and sisters, and in so doing, we reject your Love. Help us to see that these walls we build around our hearts and in our world must come tumbling down. Amen.

Deborah Kaufman Giordano

We were far away on vacation when a text came from the middle schooler charged with feeding our three cats. Disaster had struck: The house key we had left her had broken off in the lock.

Every time we made new copies of our door keys, they became less reliable, less true. Only the original worked with any kind of reliability and faithfulness. Inferior copies led to failure and frustration. Fortunately, by a miracle of modern interconnected technology, we were able to get our young pet sitter a rescue key and the cats were fed that night.

The closer we return to the original Key of David, Jesus, the safer and more secure we are. We also become more open to embracing opportunity and grace—to the nurture and comfort of God for which we hunger.

After Bethlehem, Galilee, Jerusalem—after Baby Jesus is born, grows up, outperforms all the predictions his mother ponders in her heart, is arrested and put to death—his disciples find themselves an empty room and lock the doors, fearful that what has been done to him will be done to them. No one can enter—except Jesus does. He appears in the midst of them when they are alone and grieving.

The way of life into which Jesus has been born, lives, dies, and is resurrected can never be closed, blocked off, or locked up. It has been

thrown wide open by the incarnation of God as human.
Jesus flings wide the doors of the kingdom with the original key of
David slung around his shoulder.

O come, thou Key of David, come
Open our eyes to see your glory.
Open our minds to hear your call.
Open our hearts to rejoice with your angels,
and let them never be closed against your mercy. Amen.

Rosalind C. Hughes

Wednesday

I use the garage door opener to enter and exit my house and rarely use the key to my front door. I don't even keep it on my keychain. One recent Saturday I was caring for my two young granddaughters at home. We had the best day of laughter and play. Soon, it was time for me to return the girls to their parents. We set out for the garage through an interior door. My seven-year-old granddaughter brought up the rear and closed the door behind her. As I buckled my seatbelt, she turned around and said, "I think I just locked the door by accident."

I sheepishly called the locksmith after I confirmed I had no way to re-enter my house. While I was delivering the girls to their parents, he unlocked the front door and then the back one. He even relocked my front door for safety's sake! When I returned, I walked in the house as if nothing had happened.

O Key of David, only you are worthy to open the door to the house of David. Give us grace to welcome you to the manger as you welcome us to the kingdom of God. Amen.

Leisa Phillips

Thursday

Last year, we moved to a new city. After we unpacked, I discovered that the key to an old cedar chest was missing. I tried cracking the lock with a screwdriver and pushing other keys into the lock. I even tried to bang the lid open with a hammer. Finally, I gave up and called a locksmith. Later, I found the original key inside. The movers must have had a way to lock it when they packed and then failed to open it on the other end of the move.

To open my heart in prayer, I have to admit that I need help and I don't have all the answers. My prayer may not be answered in the way that I want, and I might have to acknowledge that I need more than my own elbow grease to navigate a challenge. These are truths I prefer to ignore, and maybe you do too. Self-sufficiency is our worst illusion, an idol that rivals the golden calf.

But the key to life has been tucked inside us all along. We receive all that we need at baptism. Often, fear and shame block us from remembering that the door to the kingdom can be opened at any time. Jesus, the precious Key of David, connects us to this truth.

O Jesus Christ, O Key of David, open our hearts to your love. Amen.

Sara Irwin

Friday

Tucked away in a corner of the British Museum is a five-foot long block of limestone. Discovered in 1870 just outside Jerusalem, it was so badly damaged that the Hebrew inscription on it could not be read until 1952. Eventually archaeologists were able to ascertain that the limestone was from the doorway of the rock-cut tomb of Judah's royal steward; the grave marker ends on a cynical note: "Cursed be the man who opens this [tomb]."

Archaeologists feel confident that the man who was buried behind this block was a person named Shebna, the steward of the royal palace during the reign of King Hezekiah. Isaiah's twenty-second chapter records Shebna's downfall. Shebna was stripped of his position as royal steward and replaced by Eliakim, son of Hilkiah. Eliakim would have a glorious career, trusted by the people of Jerusalem and wielding the keys to the royal palace.

It is no surprise that Shebna faded into obscurity. It's equally unsurprising that Christians have seen Isaiah's promise to Eliakim as foreshadowing Jesus Christ. The Messiah holds the keys to the kingdom.

God, I take comfort that Jesus is the key of David. Help me to trust that even when life may feel out of control, Jesus holds me in his care. Amen.

Andrew Garnett

Saturday

When we bought our house, the previous owners had left half a dozen keys dangling above the kitchen counters. The purposes of some were obvious—one was attached to a tag that said "garage," and lo, it fit the garage door. Others fit doors we seldom use, and still others apparently unlock doors we haven't yet discovered. Those keys still hang on their hooks, less because I believe we'll ever actually need them than because their dark, weighty iron is interesting to see and pleasurable to hold. And I like believing there's more to be discovered, even about something as familiar as my own home.

That's one thing my faith teaches me: There's always more to be discovered. As a member of a community of believers, a communion of saints, a collage of images of God, I belong to the world I can see and a world I cannot yet see. I relish both the concrete and the mystical, and God opens both to me, creating me of flesh and breathing spirit into my being.

Someday, my lungs will no longer inhale, my heart will no longer beat, and my brain will no longer send or receive electrical impulses. My life, some will say, will be over. Except it won't be. In our bodily form, we are connected to all who have come before—Ruth, Boaz, David, Bathsheba, Solomon, Mary, Joseph, Jesus, our own grandparents and parents. We are connected to all who have come before us and all who will come after us, those we might suspect are saints today, those we haven't yet identified as saints. Jesus—born, died, and risen—has shown us how God inhabits that mystical life whose door is never closed.

God of life,
we are fully alive
only in you.
Keep us faithful,
confident that the keys
you hold out to us
open doors of abundance
and joy
and peace.
Amen.

Lynn Domina

O KEY OF DAVID, you open and no one closes; you close and no one opens: Come and liberate us from captivity to our past, that we may face your future's promise with boldness and purpose; through the One whom we know as the Son of David, Jesus Christ our Lord. Amen.

Advent 4

DAWN of the EAST, brightness of light eternal and Sun of justice: come and enlighten those who sit in darkness and in the shadow of death.

Sunday

❧ ❍ ❧

But there will be no gloom for those who were in anguish. In the former time he brought into contempt the land of Zebulun and the land of Naphtali, but in the latter time he will make glorious the way of the sea, the land beyond the Jordan, Galilee of the nations. The people who walked in darkness have seen a great light; those who have lived in deep darkness—on them light has shined. Isaiah 9:1-2

On Easter Eve, the service begins in darkness, a church illumined by a single candle. The Paschal Candle—symbol of Jesus Christ—burns brightly. For a moment, it is the only light. Our eyes have adjusted to the darkness, and so we see that one candle brightens the entire church. Shadows take flight.

If a single candle can shine throughout an entire church, imagine how much more the Light of Christ shines throughout our world. Though our world can seem gloomy, the Light of Christ pierces the darkness. Shadows take flight.

Without the light, we are shrouded in gloom, lost among the shadows. With the Light, we see the radiant glory of God. We do not need to fear the darkness, because the Light illumines us. Let us pray for the Light to come among us, to show us the way and to quiet our fears.

Scott Gunn

Monday

❧ ✺ ❧

What does it feel like to walk in darkness? Sometimes, I turn all the lights out and see if I can navigate through the house. Two things usually happen. I bump into something and feel pain. But I also find that if I wait long enough, my eyes adjust to the darkness and I can see more clearly.

The cycle of life holds the night and day—there is darkness and light. In the cycle of life for God's people, there are concrete moments when we turn away from God and experience loss, suffering, and death. It is in this reality that the words of Isaiah come to the people of God, reminding us that seeing the light is not a one-time event. God promises, over and over again, a way out of the anguish, despair, and darkness.

For Isaiah, light is a sign of redemption, vindication, and salvation. Light always comes in the morning and so the people of God are reminded to be faithful even in the most difficult times. I am reminded of a man who was looking for a key on a busy block. A friend of his came by and decided to help. After helping him for an hour, the friend asked where he had lost the key. The man pointed ten blocks away. "Why are we looking here?" asked the friend. The man replied, "There is more light here."

The darkness on life's journey turns out to be an invitation to expect light. Darkness can remind us that light is on the way and that there is an alternative to darkness. We are called to remember that God says, "Let there be light." The light that God gives is not magical. Following or seeking the light is all about our choosing to follow and to love God with all our mind, heart, and soul—about putting our hearts and desires in God's keeping and making God's will our own.

To see the light is not a one-time life event. To see the light calls us to walk in the light. To expect the light, we must live and seek the light. To expect the light, we must remember that God is light.

Purify our conscience, Almighty God, by your daily visitation, that your Son Jesus Christ, at his coming, may find in us a mansion prepared for himself; who lives and reigns with you, in the unity of the Holy Spirit, one God, now and for ever. Amen.

The Book of Common Prayer

Mark Bozzuti-Jones

Tuesday

A while ago, I had the opportunity to spend several weeks in the mountains of Haiti, in a village that is home to a small convent of Catholic nuns. One of my favorite things was to sit outside the convent at sunrise. While many folks were still asleep, I listened to the sisters sing their morning prayers. From total darkness, the sky began to lighten. Then, as the sun crested the mountains, the first rays of light washed over the landscape. Finally, the sun rose and brought in a new day.

Isaiah draws on the image of a rising sun to help illustrate the ways God will dispel the darkness facing the children of Israel. Zebulun and Naphtali are two tribes of Israel. Both of these tribes suffer mightily from Assyrian invasions. Isaiah promises that conditions will improve; the night may be dark, but dawn will inevitably come. God's people will not be forgotten.

God's will is not just to lift darkness in one time and place, but everywhere. God's desire sends a savior who drives away all darkness. That dawn broke in Bethlehem 2,000 years ago, and the rising of the savior's sun continues until the day Jesus himself will be a sun for us. Though our night may feel dark, dawn is breaking—and no darkness is powerful enough to stop the rising of the sun.

God, I thank you for sending us the light of the world. We pray for the day when that light will drive all darkness from our hearts, our lives, and our world, so that we might rest fully in you. Amen.

Andrew Garnett

Wednesday

The Vesper Light can be seen from historic Mount Nebo, as it shines over the Jordan River Valley in Israel.

Almighty God, we give you thanks for surrounding us, as daylight fades, with the brightness of the vesper light; and we implore you of your great mercy that, as you enfold us with the radiance of this light, so you would shine into our hearts the brightness of your Holy Spirit; through Jesus Christ our Lord. Amen.   *The Book of Common Prayer*

Furman Buchanan

Thursday

Our sun, 93 million miles away from us, might seem incapable of bringing life-giving and sustaining warmth across such a great distance. And yet, the light is so powerful that it reaches earth in a matter of seconds, with the sun consistently rising and setting day after day, warming us and allowing us to see, grow, and thrive.

To the children of Israel, God may seem millions of miles away, too far away to matter much. They feel just as broken and fearful as we do now. Isaiah conveys God's promise of a great light that will break through the deep darkness of their lives and restore them to their place of promise. God is never too far away and never too busy.

The light of God can seem so far away as to be completely absent, as though we have slipped God's mind. But when we look a little deeper into our lives and hearts, we find God's light there. When we encourage one another and when we sacrifice for one another, the light shines brightly and God's goodness and love are revealed in glory.

O Rising Sun, shine down on us. Across space and time, keep reminding us of your presence deep within our hearts. We are ever grateful for your light; may it burn forever and unquenched through our prayers and in our love for one another. Amen.

Elizabeth Floyd

Friday

Cursillo, a renewal weekend focused around Christian practice, study, and action, utilizes talks, meditations, singing, and prayer to frame the weekend. Although I had been a practicing Christian since the age of four and was baptized at ten, my true conversion—my new birth—occurred when I attended a Cursillo weekend in 1979. The theme song of that weekend was "I Want to Walk as a Child of the Light."

Like today's antiphon, this familiar hymn hinges on the interplay between darkness and light. The scriptures are replete with this juxtaposition of opposites from the moment God separates the light from the darkness; it is no accident that O Oriens is the antiphon sung on December 21, the shortest day and longest night of the year.

As I associate my own spiritual birth with a song and a metaphor of light, I have discovered the same thread when pondering death in places of apparent darkness. Traveling throughout the southern United States to photograph remnants of nineteenth-century, rural garden cemeteries, I have found abiding joy in the midst of sorrowful places, peace in the chaos of interrupted, upended lives, and in the darkest moments of human loss, the "brightness of light eternal." In the burial liturgy found in *The Book of Common Prayer*, we pray, "Grant to them eternal rest. Let light perpetual shine upon them."

Nowhere in my work has the truth of this paradox been made clearer than in the image that accompanies this meditation. I took the photograph at the grave of Kate Cooper Woolvin (1858–1895) at Oakdale Cemetery in Wilmington, North Carolina; I have entitled it "Light Perpetual."

Be our light in the darkness, O Lord, and in your great mercy defend us from all perils and dangers of this night; for the love of your only Son, our Savior Jesus Christ. Amen.

The Book of Common Prayer

Vicki Bozzola Derka

Saturday

In November 2016, I experienced a darkness that continued to grow... In creating the mosaic, I began to see cracks in the dark that let the light in. Earlier this week, we marked the winter solstice–the shortest day and longest night of the year. I intentionally created a work that requires one to see, to look closely for the light in the

darkness. The same feels true in the world around me, and I pray
for the Light of God to shine on all who sit in darkness.

O gracious light,
pure brightness of the everliving Father in heaven,
O Jesus Christ, holy and blessed!

Now as we come to the setting of the sun,
and our eyes behold the vesper light,
we sing your praises, O God: Father, Son, and Holy Spirit.

You are worthy at all times to be praised by happy voices,
O Son of God, O Giver of Life,
and to be glorified through all the worlds.
Amen.

The Book of Common Prayer

Kathy Thaden

Christmas Eve

❧ o ❧

The darkness that was breaking me was too deep.
I felt like a child hiding under the bed
hoping the scary things would not find me.
And then the bed was gone, and the room and the house vanished too.
Nothing was left but my broken places beneath dark clouds
that looked like monsters and grew as big as the haunted sky,
inhaling all of the light I was trying so desperately to breathe,
leaving only an incurable silence behind.
A silence that promised to last forever.
Until Jesus spoke.
Spoke to me with everything Jesus could think of using
to tell me the truth about my child of God self.
The sound of his voice, the look in his eyes, the touch of his hands.
He gave me all of himself to reveal what the darkness tried to hide.
Jesus knelt and found every fragment of my broken places.
He knew how to fit each one of them back into place.
I had beautiful scars, like pieces of stained glass
with his healing fingerprints all over them,
miraculous colors without names or definitions,
tints and hues that the great light of Jesus could shine through me
toward others lost in their own dark storms.
Jesus made me feel like a rainbow arcing across the sky
in an aurora borealis of grace.
I'll never forget tasting the first rays of this new sunrise on my lips,
swallowing everything I could,

luminous and laughing with joy at becoming something more than I
—more than anyone but Jesus—
ever imagined possible:
Loved by God with a light of love that will never set, a light of love
that has risen eternally.
For me. For you. For us all.

*O, Jesus, thank you for the redeeming light of your love. Help us to
incline our heart, our mind, and our soul toward you so that you
may shine that light through our own acts of compassion toward
those who are also lost in darkness. Amen.*

Ken Woodley

O RISING DAWN, you chase away the shadows of the night: Come and enlighten our darkness with visions of reconciliation, that we who are alienated one from another may seek fullness of life together; through the One whom we know as the Light of the world, Jesus Christ our Lord. Amen.

Christmas

KING of the Nations, and their desired One, the Cornerstone that makes both one: Come and deliver us, whom you have formed out of the dust of the earth.

Christmas Day

In days to come the mountain of the LORD's house shall be established as the highest of the mountains, and shall be raised above the hills; all the nations shall stream to it. Many peoples shall come and say, "Come, let us go up to the mountain of the LORD, to the house of the God of Jacob; that he may teach us his ways and that we may walk in his paths." For out of Zion shall go forth instruction, and the word of the LORD from Jerusalem. He shall judge between the nations, and shall arbitrate for many peoples; they shall beat their swords into plowshares, and their spears into pruning hooks; nation shall not lift up sword against nation, and neither shall they learn war anymore.

Isaiah 2:2–4

You probably know the famous chorus from Handel's *Messiah*, "For unto us a child is born, unto us a son is given: and the government shall be upon his shoulder: and his name shall be called Wonderful, Counselor, the mighty God, the everlasting Father, the Prince of Peace."

That's from the ninth chapter of Isaiah. It imagines a ruler who will govern with justice and peace. Isaiah's vision imagines a righteous sovereign who will be mightier even than governments. Couple that with a verse from chapter 64 of Isaiah, "Yet, O Lord, you are our Father; we are the clay, and you are our potter; we are all the work of your hand."

Reading these two aspects of Isaiah's vision together begins to square with the Jesus we know. He didn't rule with a sword. Rather, he is the Son of the Most High God. Our Maker brought us into this world, and our Redeemer frees us from sin. Armies may rise and fall, but they cannot redeem us.

In that way, Jesus is mightier than every ruler, stronger than every nation. For he alone judges the righteous and the unrighteous. Christ alone brings salvation, freedom, healing, and peace.

Scott Gunn

December 26

On my daily commute into downtown Houston, I pass the iconic "BE SOMEONE" railroad trestle bridge. Many cargo trains pass over the busy highway, on their way to delivering goods to destinations beyond. Over the years, this sign has been both the creation of artists/vandals and the target of vandals/artists. Lots of pictures are taken of these turquoise words, people with arms stretched wide, dreams in their eyes and hope in their hearts.

The words "BE SOMEONE" mean something to the people of Houston, especially in the wake of Hurricane Harvey, which brought flood waters too close to the bottom of those words. We've risen from the floodwaters stronger, and as we continued to grow, I hope each of us is taking the words to heart, to be a person who matters, whose contributions count.

One morning I drove past the words and noticed a new splash of orange paint. Someone had defaced the BE SOMEONE sign, splattering paint right through the middle of it. My creative brain began an internal squabble about why some people seem bent on destruction and the undoing of things.

I lamented to myself: *Can't something stay the same? Do you have to destroy one of our favorite spots? Didn't Harvey take enough? Can't we just get along?"* After several days of zooming by the bridge and stewing over the sign, a new thought hit me. Through the windshield and the rain, I read the words again. I realized the sign was perhaps not ruined but perhaps re-created. The orange paint covered up the word "some," and the trestle bridge now read, "BE ONE."

As I passed the bridge, I heard the phrase from the Prayers of the People in *The Book of Common Prayer*: "Father, we pray for your holy catholic Church; That we all may be one." Given the fractured times, both in our local communities and around the world, the message to "Be One" spoke volumes to my heart.

For the work of re-creation and the wisdom to see your hand in the struggle to "Be One," Lord, hear our prayer. Amen.

KariAnn Lessner

December 27

Although we're often reminded that Jesus never was and never will be the traditional king long expected by so many, it is immeasurably comforting to think of him as a mighty, conquering ruler. Watching and listening tearfully to the news of the last few months, I have reminded myself of the central truth of Isaiah's second chapter: God is still God, our constant companion, and reigning above all worldly leaders. God is sovereign over all nations and all people.

Our God also reigns in the smaller words and deeds of everyday life. Focusing on the subtler moments of grace in our lives reveals the supremacy and constancy of God's kingdom. God teaches us through Bible study and prayerful meditation, arbitrates through the application of compassion and understanding, and moves us to reconcile ourselves to one another in humility. There is no need for swords or spears, no need for war.

Eternal God, in whose perfect kingdom no sword is drawn but the sword of righteousness, no strength known but the strength of love: So mightily spread abroad your Spirit, that all peoples may be gathered under the banner of the Prince of Peace, as children of one Father, to whom be dominion and glory, now and for ever. Amen.
The Book of Common Prayer

Elizabeth Floyd

O KING OF THE NATIONS, you defend the cause of the poor and raise up the oppressed of the earth: Come and build us into a world community where all are valued and the vulnerable protected, through the One whom we know as the chief cornerstone, Jesus Christ our Lord. Amen.

O Emmanuel

EMMANUEL, GOD WITH US, our King and Lawgiver, the expected of the nations and their Savior: Come to save us, O Lord our God.

December 28

For a child has been born for us, a son given to us; authority rests upon his shoulders and he is named Wonderful Counselor, Mighty God, Everlasting Father, Prince of Peace. His authority shall grow continually, and there shall be endless peace for the throne of David and his kingdom. He will establish and uphold it with justice and with righteousness from this time onward and forevermore. The zeal of the LORD of hosts will do this. Isaiah 9:6-7

Immanuel and Emmanuel are two spellings for one word. God-with-us. This one word is perhaps the best encapsulation of the who, what, why, and how of Jesus Christ. He is God with us. When we sing carols about Jesus our Emmanuel, we are affirming a God who has chosen to live in solidarity with us, to experience every aspect of humanity. We are also rejecting the idea that God is remote, impossibly distant from us.

We yearn for Jesus to come among us. We long for our savior to be with us, for we know that he has loved us enough to dwell with us, to move into our neighborhood. A God who made the heavens and the earth and yet who chooses to dwell with us is remarkable, indeed. God-with-us, Jesus our Emmanuel, must truly love us.

Scott Gunn

December 29

Every moment a child is being born. This reality is an invitation to reflect on our own birth and how our life is a gift to the world. Since the beginning of time, a child has been born for us.

Whether we are a child, woman, or man, all of our births fall in line with God's plan of redemption and love for this world. Our presence in the world comes with the authority of God resting upon us. This authority is echoed in our baptisms and deepens with all the baptismal promises we make.

We don't have to be parents to be delighted by the laughter, play, words, and actions of children. Children bring us hope. By their nature, children have a way of reminding us to be kind, caring, compassionate, and loving. In this prophecy in Isaiah, the child represents the hopes and fears of a people for a time of redemption and new hope.

Yet despite the joy of children, few adults regard them as leaders. Few of us would trust that a child could offer salvation. So why does God come to us as a child? I believe God uses a child to remind us that the weak, young, and vulnerable can be powerful vessels of God's amazing grace.

God constantly calls us to reimagine reality. The mystery of Christmas is expressed through the innocence and vulnerability of an infant. When we are vulnerable and innocent and desiring God's grace, we experience the awesome nature of God acting in surprising ways. Imagining that a child can offer justice and righteousness can be a hard sell. We know that in God's economy what seems unlikely and impossible often holds the greatest truth and the surest path to redemption.

The zeal of the Lord of hosts has done this. The zeal of the Lord of hosts is doing this. The zeal of the Lord of hosts will do this. A Son is given to us. Doubt no further. Believe. Look for the child. Live like the child.

Almighty God, you have given your only-begotten Son to take our nature upon him, and to be born of a pure virgin: Grant that we, who have been born again and made your children by adoption and grace, may daily be renewed by your Holy Spirit; through our Lord Jesus Christ, to whom with you and the same Spirit be honor and glory, now and for ever. Amen.   *The Book of Common Prayer*

Mark Bozzuti-Jones

December 30

This melon is part of the third-grade Community Learning Garden at Roosevelt Elementary School in Santa Monica, California. The garden is a place where learning, respect, dignity, and peace have taken deep root and continue to grow and blossom.

Emmanuel, as you enter the world as a powerless child, you show us that the power of love overcomes the love of power. Where there is violence and war in our hearts help us to receive and to share your gift of peace. As we sow seeds of peace, let these seeds take deep root, grow continually, and burst forth with the fruit of endless peace, here in this world and the life to come. Amen.

O God, you made us in your own image and redeemed us through Jesus your Son: Look with compassion on the whole human family; take away the arrogance and hatred which infect our hearts; break down the walls that separate us; unite us in bonds of love; and work through our struggle and confusion to accomplish your purposes on earth; that, in your good time, all nations and races may serve you in harmony around your heavenly throne; through Jesus Christ our Lord. Amen.   *The Book of Common Prayer*

Deborah Kaufman Giordano

December 31

Only in retrospect do Christians sing that Jesus was the child for us. Isaiah doesn't have Jesus in mind as he writes to the beleaguered children of Israel, but Jesus is in our hearts and minds as we read this passage.

Isaiah prepares us for something unexpected. But it is always the shocking, unforeseen elements in any story, that lead us into redemptive mystery. I remember the opening scene of *Les Misérables*: A recently paroled convict—bitter, unloved, and unwanted—finds himself invited to share an elderly bishop's fire, dinner, and a place to rest. In the night, the convict, Jean Valjean, steals two silver candlesticks and escapes. Caught and forced back to the house by triumphant policemen, the bishop unexpectedly confirms the prisoner's story: He had given Valjean the candlesticks and other silver besides. The astounded police depart. Equally astounded, Valjean finds himself converted: To love. To peace. To hope.

The rest of the story hangs entirely on the truth of this unexpected conversion from darkness to light, from despair to hope, from sadness to joy, until the holy child is born again in Valjean, to the everlasting joy of those who have discovered God's magnificent mercy.

Blessed are you, O Lord, the God of our fathers, creator
of the changes of day and night, giving rest to the weary,
renewing the strength of those who are spent, bestowing

upon us occasions of song in the evening. As you have
protected us in the day that is past, so be with us in the
coming night; keep us from every sin, every evil, and every
fear; for you are our light and salvation, and the strength
of our life. To you be glory for endless ages. Amen.

The Book of Common Prayer

Minda Cox

January 1

I'm intrigued by grammar, thinking about how words fit together to create meaning—it's nerdy, I know, but it helps me when I'm reading the Bible or thinking about prayer. Lately, I've been thinking about the difference between singular and plural, between "I" and "we" or "me" and "us."

Sometimes we use "we" when we have no right to, assuming that other people's goals and values are just like our own. Perhaps I'm doing exactly that right here. Other times, we forget about others entirely, focusing only on me, me, me—God and me, Jesus and me. Praying the word Emmanuel is a reminder that the incarnation is a profound act involving the entire human community.

Emmanuel. Such a sacred title for Jesus, such a sacred name whose very root reminds us that God is with us, with us all. This knowledge is one of the most reassuring aspects of the incarnation. Emmanuel, God-with-us, reminds me that we all belong to this beloved community, all of us, no matter what..

I belong and so does the neighbor with the scraggly lawn and the other neighbor whose bumper stickers annoy me and the celebrity who behaves so badly and the friends and family members I hold dear. Emmanuel, God-with-us, all of us. I long for such an inclusive community to be made manifest. The incarnation shows us the way: Emmanuel dwelling among all of us, all of us dwelling beside

Emmanuel and beside each other: what a vision of a Wonderful Counselor, a Mighty God, an Everlasting Father, a Prince of Peace!

O Emmanuel,
be always among us,
reminding us that God
became flesh, that God
experienced hunger and cold,
warmth and satiety.
Help us to become
more generous, more welcoming,
more joyful while we dwell
with you and one another.
Amen.

Lynn Domina

January 2

This icon was the focus of an O Antiphon pre-Advent retreat. As we learned about, prayed with, and shared thoughts and images about each O Antiphon, we moved toward the seventh and final one, Emmanuel, the One who holds all names and yet is beyond a single name. The Light invites us to reflect the multiple facets of this gift of Emmanuel.

O Holy One,
Here, lonely and exiled, longing for more than rags on our backs,
we search for a way, or a key,
or some holy moment or patch of holy ground to redeem us.
And there, wrapped in swaddling clothes,
is a cry under a star,
whose hands will tend roots of hope,
whose feet will walk toward the first light,
whose voice will offer wisdom,
whose love will be poured into the world's woundedness,
and whose light will show us that
the underside of our rags is a swaddling cloth
because You desire us to be born yet again.
O Emmanuel, Veni!
O Emmanuel, Come!

Cathy Johnson

January 3

Going out in the rain in an electric wheelchair is tricky. I became anxious as the cold morning rain poured harder. I had been looking forward to attending my weekly Weight Watchers meeting, helping my artist friend teach a painting class at a nursing home, and speaking for a group of church women later in the afternoon.

I called my friend Gretchen, who happily told me that her day was free and she'd be glad to help me with transportation. But she's an older adult lady; lifting the chair and helping me get into the car worried her. But many others stepped up to fill in the gaps.

My neighbor lifted me into Gretchen's car and put my manual wheelchair and artwork in the trunk. At my first meeting, another man lifted me out of the car and into my chair—and then back in the car afterward; he cheerfully and competently put my wheelchair back in the trunk as well. The nursing home director helped us when we arrived. At the church for the women's meeting, the pastor assisted us.

The day turned out to be full of light despite the rain. It was clear to me that the glory of the Lord had indeed risen upon each of these amazing people in my life, whether they knew it or not. I could practically see glory all over us, most especially in Gretchen, who gave her entire day to make mine possible. Many people catch a glimpse of God's glory in Gretchen, who so freely responds to the call,

"Arise, shine; for your light has come!" She does it in trust and in joy, unaware of what others see.

The whole world is already aflame with the beauty of God, shining out in blazing glory. Some day we will all have eyes to see God's glory and be startled awake, recognizing that the light of the Lord has risen upon us—and upon all of creation.

Come, Lord Jesus, be Light to us. Shine on us, and shine out of us, that your glory may be revealed. Amen.

Minda Cox

January 4

I grew up in a family that eschewed Advent and went straight for a full-throttle embrace of Christmas as soon as Thanksgiving dinner was over. I cannot read this passage from Isaiah without immediately hearing the accompanying brassy trumpet peals of a monumental production of Handel's *Messiah*. They blared forth from the TV set in the living room of my childhood home as we decorated our tree, from the invisible speakers in every mall department store we trudged through in search of presents and pictures with Santa, and on the radio in the family station wagon that ferried us from school concert to family party to tree lighting in the town square.

I suspect if you stopped a stranger on the street and asked them to sing this Christmas composition, the words that they would sing right after "Hallelujah" would be: "Wonderful! Counselor!"

It is the soundtrack to Christmas, as much a part of the sensory experience of December as the sight of red velvet bows, gold glitter stars, candy cane stripes, and the smell of pine boughs. But I'm not sure we really pay attention to the meaning of the words, caught up as we are in the glory of the staging: For unto us a child is born...authority rests upon his shoulders, and his name shall be Wonderful Counselor, Mighty God, Everlasting Father, Prince of Peace.

And this is why the long, solemn days of preparation that we make in Advent are critically necessary: This is why we cannot have one without the other. By our Advent preparations of fasting and prayer, we are reminded that this entire celebration, this Christmas world of joy and bounty and gold-glitter stars, is balanced on the shoulders of a newborn child, his tiny, fragile body shivering in the night chill, his first cry ringing out into the world he was born to redeem.

Emmanuel, our King, our Savior, come to save us. Amen

Mariclair Partee Carlsen

January 5

Long before we picked up the apple, God tasked us with naming all the plants and animals. Besides being fruitful and multiplying, coming up with names for things seems to be the only other job Adam and Eve have. Of course, God spends a considerable amount of time making the world and everything in it, so they kind of have their work cut out for them. Tangentially, you and I might wonder what they called each other, what the Edenic form of Sweetie or Darling or Dear Heart might have been. Make no mistake: Names matter. What we call items, people, ideas, each other—those sweet nothings we whisper and the expletives we holler.

Tomorrow is Epiphany, the day we remember Mary and Joseph and baby Jesus being visited by kings from the East, and then fleeing to Egypt to save their lives. But for one more day, we get to sit here with this baby who has so many weighty names hanging around his tender little neck, holding up the substance of who he is long before he can balance his head. There's that little hollow at the base of his neck, a holy little divot that Mary and Joseph murmur lullabies and psalms and nonsense into when he cries, as inconsolable and pitiful as only an infant can be. Imagine holding that tiny bundle of immeasurable grace and glory, soothing the firstborn of all creation with a belly rub and a deep drink of his mama's milk.

This baby is sweetness and light, who makes your eyes well up when he nuzzles his head between your face and your shoulder, who will become a busy toddler, maddening teenager, intense 20-something, and be proclaimed the Beloved in front of his cousin John and their friends. This Jesus sits with us in this moment, being all of these things, fitting all of these names: God-with-Us, Wonderful Counselor, Mighty God, Everlasting Father, Prince of Peace. I don't have any idea how that kind of time warp works, only that it does. And the zeal of the LORD of hosts will do this.

Keep watch, dear Lord, with those who work, or watch, or weep this night, and give your angels charge over those who sleep. Tend the sick, Lord Christ; give rest to the weary, bless the dying, soothe the suffering, pity the afflicted, shield the joyous; and all for your love's sake. Amen.

The Book of Common Prayer

Rachel Jones

January 6
Feast of the Epiphany

Fifteen years ago, I led a children's service day at a local retirement center. Our group of elementary students came to bring some levity into the assisted living facility. We toted in a host of things to fill our time: bingo, balloons (for gentle games of volleyball), and lots of art supplies. After we set up stations around the room, several residents made their way into the room and settled in front of giant pieces of paper and a wild assortment of crayons.

An older woman with jet-black hair and oversized glasses shuffled up to the table and asked what I was doing. I explained that there were no specific guidelines—just to have fun. She pulled up a chair and with a voice as clear as a bell, she said, "Well, I'm going to teach you a thing or two about light and how to paint a sunrise." And with that, she drew a horizon along the middle of the page with a brown crayon. She rebuffed my black crayon, saying we'd just "make our own black if we need it." There isn't any thing that is "truly black; there's always a little color in there…a little light."

I expected her to pick up the yellow crayon next, but she didn't. She reached for the green one, explaining, "The first color in a sunrise is always green. Folks think it's yellow, but that's not right. You just watch next time you see a sunrise and see if I'm not right."

This woman knew the power of the light. Because she spoke with such authority and conviction, I was drawn to both her and the Light, exactly the way Isaiah said it would happen.

We can invite others toward the light with every interaction we undertake, every word we speak, and every seemingly insignificant moment. I wonder what would have happened if I had blown her off as "an eccentric old woman" or someone "who doesn't know what she's talking about." What would I have missed?

Aside from an amazing number of sunrises (I've been looking for the green rays ever since my visit with her), I would have missed hearing the conviction of a life spent in pursuit of the light. As we cleaned up, one of the nurses came by and said, "I'm not sure you know the woman you were sitting with, but she spent her whole life teaching art at a very well-respected college. You just got a lesson that some folks paid thousands of dollars to get. This must be your lucky day!"

This incredible woman invited me to celebrate the light with her. But her lasting work was possibly unintended; what I remember most about my time with her is how she drew me in to adore the Light of the world.

For those who draw us to your Light, and those who draw out your light in our lives: Lord, hear our prayer. Amen.

KariAnn Lessner

*O EMMANUEL, God with us, you dwell beyond our farthest reach,
yet are nearer to us than we are to ourselves: Come among us in
these days of expectation, that we may give birth to what is true, just,
beautiful, and good; for you are the One whom we know as Lord,
and with the Creator and the Holy Spirit, you abide with us, one God,
now and forever. Amen.*

Acknowledgments

Forward Movement owes a special debt of gratitude to the music and communications ministries of Saint Mark's Episcopal Cathedral in Seattle, Washington, for allowing us to reprint the bidding prayers and collects from their O Antiphon liturgy. You will find the bidding prayer at the beginning of each week and the collect at the end. These lovely prayers were composed by the Rev. Frederick "Fritz" Fritschel, retired pastor at Lutheran Church of Honolulu, Hawaii. May he rest in peace and rise in glory.

We are also indebted to Mimi Heldman and Sally Chambers for their lovely woodcuts, which anchored each week of the O Antiphons. Mimi Heldman is an artist in Nashville, Tennessee, and a member of St. Bartholomew's Episcopal Church. Sally Chambers is the director of communications for St. Bartholomew's in Nashville.

About the Contributors

Furman Buchanan is the rector of St. Peter's Episcopal Church in Greenville, South Carolina. He is a firm believer that the mission of Jesus cannot be understood apart from the prophesy of Isaiah, whom Jesus himself quoted to describe his life's purpose.

Mariclair Partee Carlsen lives with her husband and two daughters in Philadelphia, where she is the rector of St. Mary's, Hamilton Village, and the Episcopal chaplain to the University of Pennsylvania.

Bill Carroll is the canon for clergy transitions and congregational life in the Diocese of Oklahoma. He is married to Tracey Carroll, with whom he has two children.

Minda Cox is an artist, activist, and contributing writer for Forward Movement living in Bolivar, Missouri. A lifelong Episcopalian, Minda worships with the community of St. Alban's Episcopal Church in Bolivar.

Lynn Domina is a poet living in Marquette, Michigan, where she is a member of St. Paul's Episcopal Church. She serves as head of the English department at Northern Michigan University and as creative writing editor of *The Other Journal.*

Vicki Bozzola Derka teaches freshman composition at the community-college level. She worships at St. Michael's Episcopal Church in Raleigh, North Carolina.

Donna Z. Falcone is a writer, alcohol ink artist, and illustrator of the children's book *A is for Azure: The Alphabet in Colors*. Donna lives in Tifton, Georgia, and is a member of Saint Anne's Episcopal Church.

Alyssa Finke serves as the marketing coordinator for Forward Movement. Alyssa and her partner Isaiah make their home in Cincinnati, Ohio.

Elizabeth Floyd is the coordinator of Christian formation at Church of the Resurrection in Greenwood, South Carolina. She lives with her husband, three children, and Marley the dog.

Andrew Garnett is a minister at Forest Hills Baptist Church in Raleigh, North Carolina. He enjoys spending time with his wife and daughter, hiking, visiting historical sites, and playing board games.

Deborah Kaufman Giordano is a healthcare marketing and communications recruiter and a member of St. Augustine By-The-Sea Episcopal Church in Santa Monica, California.

Scott Gunn is the executive director at Forward Movement in Cincinnati, Ohio. He is the human of George T. Dog, the unofficial canine mascot of *Forward Day by Day*. You can read Scott's blog at www.sevenwholedays.org.

Christine Havens loves to play with words and ideas residing in Austin, Texas and doing parish work with St. Matthew's Episcopal Church. She has master's degrees in English and religion. Her blog can be found at www.ripplesinthefont.com.

Rosalind C. Hughes is the rector of the Church of the Epiphany, Euclid, Ohio.

Sara Irwin is an Episcopal priest living in Pittsburgh, Pennsylvania. She is mom to Isaiah and Adah and spouse to Noah Evans, rector of St. Paul's Episcopal Church in Mount Lebanon. She loves tattoos, hiking, and making beer. Her blog is at saraiwrites.blogspot.com.

Cathy Johnson is an ordained Presbyterian pastor currently serving as a chaplain with the Adrian Dominican Sisters.

Mark Bozzuti-Jones is a priest and the director of core values and Latin American and Caribbean partnerships at Trinity Episcopal Church in New York City.

Rachel Jones is the associate editor for Forward Movement. She and her husband—and a menagerie of animals—live on a farm in Northern Kentucky.

Marguerite Kirchhoff is affiliated with the Order of Julian of Norwich and worships at Nativity Episcopal Church in Burnsville, Minnesota.

KariAnn Lessner is the minister for children and families at Christ Church Cathedral in Houston, Texas. Married to Ron, with whom she has two amazing and rapidly growing humans, KariAnn also cohosts "You Brew You," a podcast about female friendships and the miracles of ministry.

Pamela A. Lewis is a retired French teacher and a member of St. Thomas Church in New York City. She writes for *The Episcopal New Yorker* and *Episcopal Journal*.

Stephanie London is an Anglican priest in Sherwood Park, Alberta, Canada. She is passionate about exploring the visual theology of the church and helping people express their spirituality creatively.

Leisa Phillips is a music educator and church musician. She is a member of St. John's Episcopal Church in Harrison, Arkansas, where she serves as lector and eucharistic minister.

Kathy Thaden's mosaics range from abstract sculpture and landscapes to liturgical art and commissioned works. Kathy is founder and former president of Colorado Mosaic Artists. She is an active member of St. John Chrysostom Episcopal Church in Golden, Colorado, where her husband, Tim, serves as rector. See more of her work at www.thadenmosaics.com

Richelle Thompson serves as the deputy director and managing editor for Forward Movement in Cincinnati, Ohio. A professional Episcopal communicator for two decades, Richelle is dedicated to sharing the gospel and uniting people through stories. She and her family make their home in Northern Kentucky where her husband is the rector of St. Andrew's Episcopal Church.

Ken Woodley is a licensed lay preacher in the Episcopal Church at St. Anne's in Appomattox, Virginia. Ken is the author of *A Civil Rights Reparations Story: The Road to Healing in Prince Edward County, Virginia.*

About Forward Movement

Forward Movement is committed to inspiring disciples and empowering evangelists. Our ministry is lived out by creating resources such as books, small-group studies, apps, and conferences. Our daily devotional, *Forward Day by Day*, is also available in Spanish (*Adelante Día a Día*) and Braille, online, as a podcast, and as an app for smartphones or tablets. It is mailed to more than fifty countries, and we donate nearly 30,000 copies each quarter to prisons, hospitals, and nursing homes.

We actively seek partners across the church and look for ways to provide resources that inspire and challenge. A ministry of the Episcopal Church for over eighty years, Forward Movement is a nonprofit organization funded by sales of resources and by gifts from generous donors.

To learn more about Forward Movement and our resources, visit www.ForwardMovement.org. We are delighted to be doing this work and invite your prayers and support.